Course   Cursive Handwriting
Grades 3-6

http://create.mheducation.com

ISBN-10: 1264402325   ISBN-13: 9781264402328

1 LMN 20

McGraw-Hill Reading

Wonders

Handwriting

Aa Bb Cc Dd
Ee Ff Gg Hh

Mc
Graw
Hill

Table of Contents

The Manuscript Alphabet Review

Circle the letters that spell the name of your state.

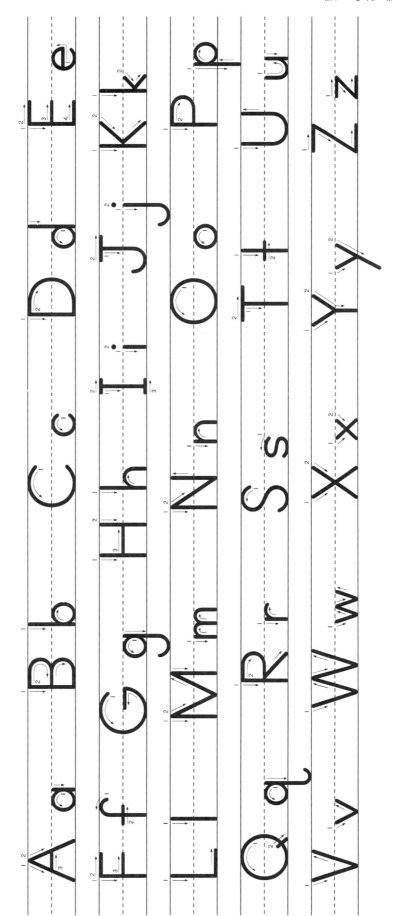

Name _____

Date _____

Lines in Letters

Write these letters with straight lines. Then use them to write a word.

E t H F i L I

Write these letters with slant lines.

A y W v k M x

Write these letters with circle lines.

S b D Q o a e

Complete the sentence.

My favorite color is

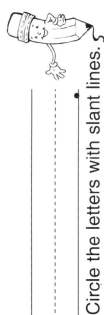

Circle the letters with slant lines.

Name _____ Date _____

Letter and Word Spacing

Space Between Letters

- not too close
- not too far apart
- space of a pencil point between letters

too close

too far

notlikethis

Space Between Words

- not too close
- space of a pencil between words

just right

likethis

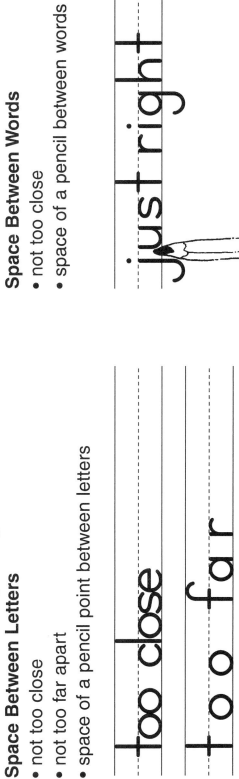

Name _____

Date _____

Numerals and Punctuation Marks

Trace and write the words and numerals.

1   one

2   two

3   three

4   four

5   five

6   six

7   seven

8   eight

9   nine

10 ten

Trace the punctuation marks.

. ? ! . ? ! . ? !

Write this sentence:

My cat has 5 kittens!

Name _____

Date _____

Writing Sentences

Write the sentences. Remember to include the correct punctuation.

The world has many endangered

animals. The Asian tiger is one.

The California condor is another.

What can be done to help?

Name _____

Date _____

Signing Up

Fill out the form. Write as neatly as you can.

Sports Club Membership Form

Name: _____

Address: _____
_____
_____

Grade and Class: _____

Interests: _____
_____
_____

Name _____

Date _____

Left-Handed Writers

Cursive Writing Position

Sit tall. Place both arms on the table.
Keep your feet flat on the floor.

Slant your paper.

Hold the pencil with your first two fingers
and your thumb.

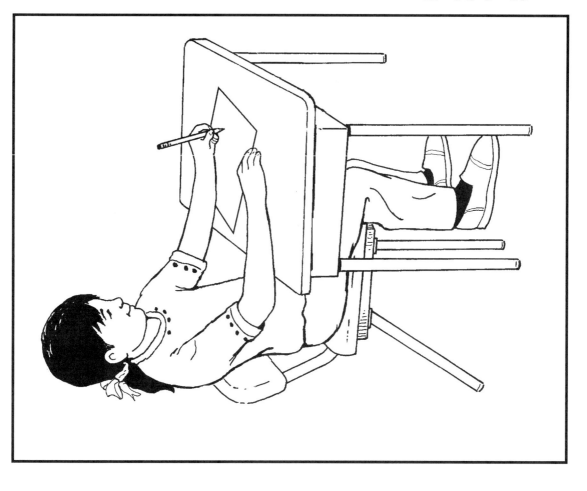

Name _____ Date _____

Right-Handed Writers

Sit tall. Place both arms on the table.
Keep your feet flat on the floor.

Slant your paper.

Hold the pencil with your first two fingers
and your thumb.

Cursive Writing Position

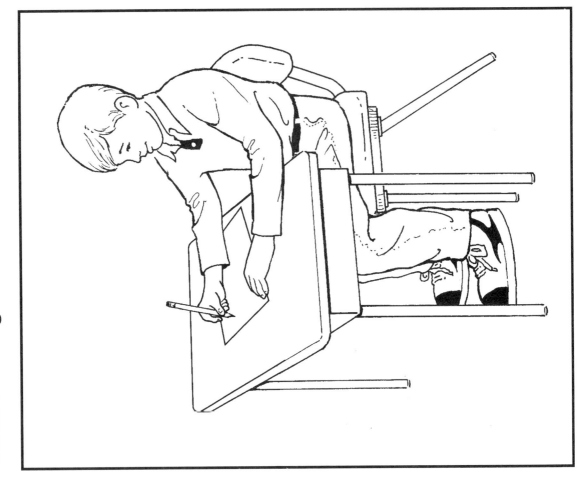

Manuscript to Cursive

Circle the cursive letters that are in your first name.

| a | a | b | b | c | c | d | d | e | e | f | f | g | g |

| h | h | i | i | j | j | k | k | l | l | m | m |

| n | n | o | o | p | p | q | q | r | r | s | s | t | t |

| u | u | v | v | w | w | x | x | y | y | z | z |

Look at the word in manuscript. Circle the matching word in cursive.

| apply | doggy | apply | oddly |

| much | macho | macho | much |

| black | black | flash | dark |

Name _____ Date _____

Circle the cursive letters that begin the names of your favorite characters.

Aa Bb Cc Dd Ee Ff Gg

Hh Ii Jj Kk Ll Mm

Nn Oo Pp Qq Rr Ss

Tt Uu Vv Ww Xx Yy Zz

Write the beginning letters of the months of the year in manuscript and in cursive.

_ _

_____

_____

_ _

Name _____

Date _____

The Cursive Alphabet

a b c d e f g h i

j k l m n o p q

r s t u v w x y z

A B C D E F G

H I J K L M N

O P Q R S T U

V W X Y Z

Name _____ Date _____

Size and Shape

Tall letters touch the top line

h d l t

Short letters touch the middle line.

o a n m c w w

These letters go below the bottom line.

g f p y p y

Circle the letters that are the right size and shape and sit on the bottom line.

u w n d g p
e l b g o f m c

Name _____

Date _____

Review

Write the cursive words in manuscript.

journey over towering ran

scattered exit quick zip

January February March

Write a word you can write in cursive.

_____

Name _____ Date _____

Taking Tests
Write **True** or **False** to answer each question.

1. Manuscript and cursive letters all look alike. _____

2. In cursive handwriting, letters are connected. _____

3. In manuscript handwriting, letters should not be too close. _____

4. Names of people begin with lowercase letters. _____

Trace and write each letter. Circle your best cursive and manuscript letter.

Name _____ Date _____

Taking Tests

Complete each sentence. Choose a word from the word bank.

Word Bank				
circle	top	straight	uppercase	slant	middle

1. The manuscript letters t, E, H, L, F, and I have _____ _____ lines.

2. Tall cursive letters touch the _____ _____ line.

3. The manuscript letters Q, D, o, a, and e have _____ _____ lines.

4. Short cursive letters touch the _____ line.

5. The manuscript letters A, M, w, v, and Y have _____ _____ lines.

6. Your first and last names begin with _____ letters.

Name _____

_____ Date

Strokes that Curve Up

Circle each letter whose beginning stroke curves up.

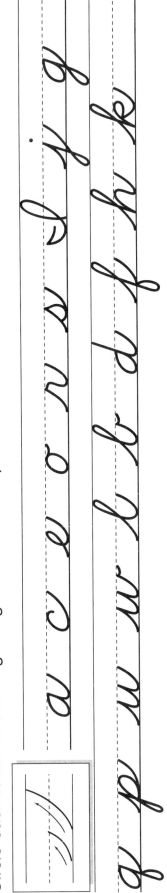

Trace and write the strokes that curve up.

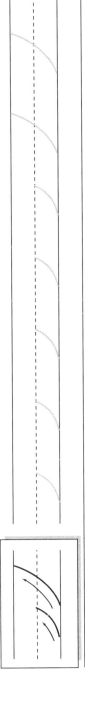

Trace the beginning stroke in each letter. Then write words using the letters.

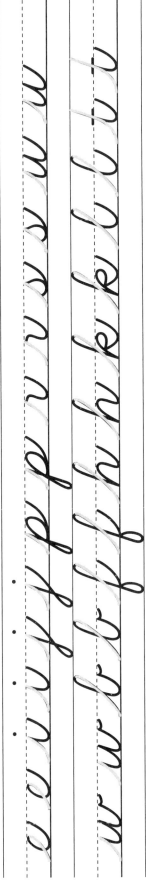

Name _____

i t

Trace and write the letters. Then trace and write the word.

Grade 3, Unit 2

Name _____

e l

Trace and write the letters. Then write the words.

e

l

ill lit tie let tile

Name _____

Date _____

Words to Write
Write the words.

Circle your best words.

tell   title   tie   it

tell   title   tie   it

let   tilt   lie   little

Write a silly title for a book. Use some of the words above.

_____

_____

Name _____ Date _____

Strokes that Curve Down

Circle each letter whose beginning stroke curves down.

Trace and write strokes that curve down.

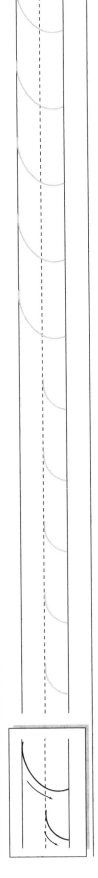

Trace the beginning stroke in each letter.

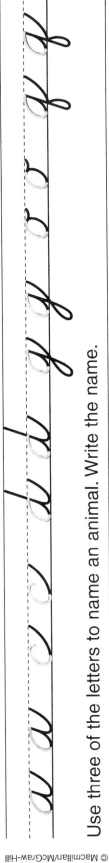

Use three of the letters to name an animal. Write the name.

_____

Name _____   Date _____

o a

Trace and write the letters. Then write the words.

$\mathcal{O}$

a

toe toll toil tail ate

tote late oil oat lot

Name _____   Date _____

c d

Trace and write the letters. Then write the words and the phrases.

c c c c c

d d d d d

coat   deed   load   code

moon dance   note time

Name _____ Date _____

Strokes that Curve Over

Circle each letter whose beginning stroke curves over.

a b c d e f g h i j

k l m n o p w r x y g

Trace and write strokes that curve over.

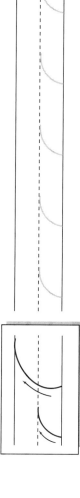

Trace the beginning stroke in each letter.

m m m m n n n n

y y y f f f f

Write words that begin with strokes that curve over.

Name _____

n m
Trace and write the letters. Then write the words.

n n

m m

name   note   moat   mitten

tame   mail   melt   mine

Date _____

Review

Write the strokes that curve up.

Write strokes that curve down.

Write strokes that curve over.

Write slant strokes.

Name _____ Date _____

Review

Write the words.
Do your tall letters touch the top line? Do your letters slant correctly?

dime   needle   meal   unite

beetle   wombat   bobcat

wooden   undid   fence

bow-wow   meow   ladle

Name _____ Date _____

Taking Tests

Write phrases in cursive to answer each question.
Choose a phrase from the answer box.

Answer Box
a stroke that curves down   all the letters   the top line
with strokes that curve up   the letters m and n

1. How do the lowercase letters **i** and **t** begin?

- -

2. What kind of stroke is at the beginning of lowercase letter **a**?

- -

3. Which letters in the word *moon* begin with a stroke that curves over?

- -

4. Which letters in the word *list* begin with a stroke that curves up?

- -

5. What line do all tall letters touch?

- -

Name _____

_____ Date _____

Connectives
Trace the connectives.

air tie her met like

an and end in sand

glad just yell zebra games

you by yarn gap lazy jam

five pick feel quite plan

u w

Trace and write the letters. Then write the words.

u

w

wait writ could would

unm undo uncle lute

Name _____ Date _____

b f

Trace and write the letters. Then write the words and the phrases.

b

f

boat   fall   bubble   off

fine food   bat and ball

Name _____

Date _____

h k

Trace and write the letters. Then write the words.

h   *h*   *h*   *h*

k   *k*   *k*   *k*

chick   *hatch*   *kickball*

hook   *kilt*   *luck*   *kite*

Name _____

Date _____

g q
Trace and write the letters. Then write the phrases.

_g_ _g_

_q_ _q_

quacked good and loud

quite a fog

Name _____ Date _____

j p

Trace and write the letters. Then write the phrases.

j

p

pound a beat   pull up

to put on an act

Name _____ Date _____

r s

Trace and write the letters. Then write the phrases.

r

s

pride and joy   set sail

rose blossom   rings a bell

Name _____

y z

Trace and write the letters. Then write the phrases.

y

z

zip code   zoom in

pretty yellow azaleas

Name _____

v x

Trace and write the letters. Then write the phrases.

v   *v*

x   *x*

x marks the spot

vim and vigor

Name _____   Date _____

Review

Trace and write the phrases. Most of the 26 letters are included.

very huge signs on bus

puppy at the end gone

quickly at second exit

are going home with jam

Circle your best letter.

Name _____

Date _____

Practice

Trace these connectives. Then write the words.

ball oats ran wait boat

bird once very when

cut its day nut can

join yard flash pick

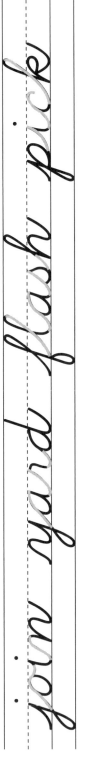

Circle your best joining.

Name _____ Date _____

Taking Tests

Write a sentence to answer each question.

1. How do you begin a sentence?

_ _

_____

_ _

2. What kind of cursive letters begin the months of the year?

_ _

_____

_ _

3. What is the difference between the cursive uppercase letters **T** and **F**?

_ _

_____

_ _

Size and Shape

All uppercase letters are tall letters.
Tall letters should touch the top line.

Letters with descenders go below the bottom line.

You can make your writing easy to read.

Look at the letters below. Circle the letters that
are the correct size and shape.

Name _____

A O

Trace and write the letters. Then write the sentences.

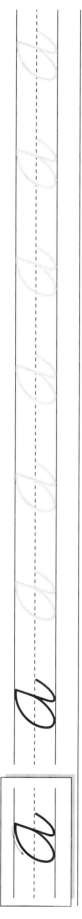

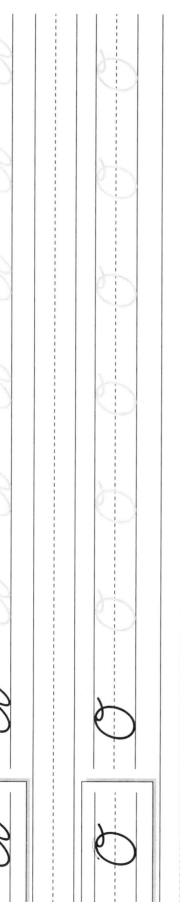

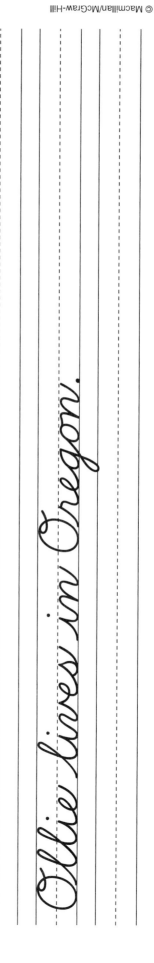

Alice lives in Alaska.

Ollie lives in Oregon.

Name _____

C E

Trace and write the letters. Then write the sentences.

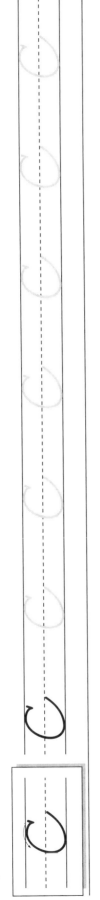

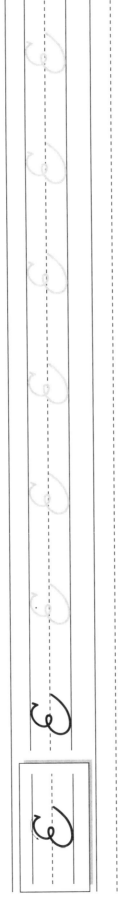

Cecily wants to visit China.

Edward went to England.

L D

Trace and write the letters. Then write the sentences.

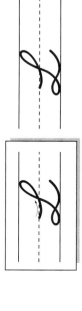

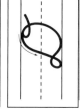
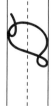
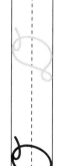

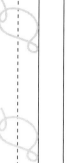
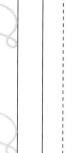

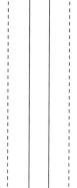
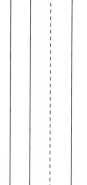

Dad asked Dina to dance.

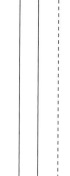
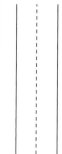

Leo dined at Dina's house.

Name _____

Date _____

B R

Trace and write the letters. Then write the sentences.

$\mathcal{B}$ $\mathcal{B}$

$\mathcal{R}$ $\mathcal{R}$

$\mathit{Bess\ bought\ a\ Brazilian\ bird.}$

$\mathit{Rick\ can\ read\ some\ Russian.}$

Name _____   Date _____

T F

Trace and write the letters. Then write the sentences.

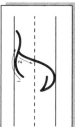

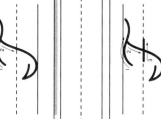

Theodore Roosevelt won.

Franklin D. Roosevelt won, too.

Name _____

Date _____

S G

Trace and write the letters. Then write the sentences.

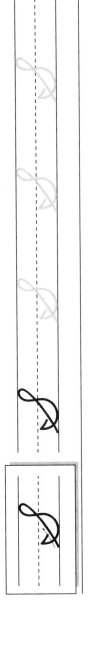

Sue sees Glen on Saturday.

Señora Gomez is the guest.

Name _____

I J

Trace and write the letters. Then write the sentences.

I

J

Ida is cooking Indian food.

Jack cooks a Jamaican dish.

Name _____

Date _____

Review

Copy the sentences.

Remember to space letters and words evenly.

Do you know the capitals?

Tallahassee, Florida

Atlanta, Georgia

Salt Lake City, Utah

Name _____ Date _____

Practice

Copy the poster. Write in manuscript. Which writing works best?

Come One, Come All

Gymnastics Tryouts ✳ *Everyone Welcome*

Tuesday at 3:00 ✳ *in the gym*

Trampoline, tumbling, bars, rings

✳   ✳

Name _____

Taking Tests
Use your best cursive handwriting to fill in the short paragraph that answers the test question. Choose words from the Word Bank.

Test Question: Why is it important to write cursive letters correctly?

Correctly written

letters are easy to _____

_____.

They can make

sentences clear. Unclear

words might _____ the

wrong message.

Name _____ Date _____

Taking Tests

Write an explanation in your best cursive handwriting.

Test Question: Which writing works best when you write a note to a friend? Explain your answer.

I think writing in cursive works best when I write a note because I can write it faster. Cursive writing also makes the note very personal.

Copy the explanation in the box or write your own.

_____

- -

_____

- -

_____

- -

_____

- -

_____

Name _____ Date _____

Spacing Letters and Words

You can make your writing easy to read.
Letters should not be too close or too far apart.

These letters are spaced

just right.

Draw a slanted line between these words to check
that the spacing is as wide as a small o.

Then copy the sentences.

The flowers are in bloom.

Can you smell the flowers?

Name _____

M N

Trace and write the letters. Then write the sentences.

m *m* *m* *m* *m* *m* *m* *m*

n *n* *n* *n* *n* *n* *n* *n*

Minnesota, North Dakota, and

Montana are in the midwest.

Name _____

H K

Trace and write the letters. Then write the sentences.

Hank and Kitty like Hanover.

Kyle lives in Kentucky.

Name _____   Date _____

P Q

Trace and write the letters. Then write the words.

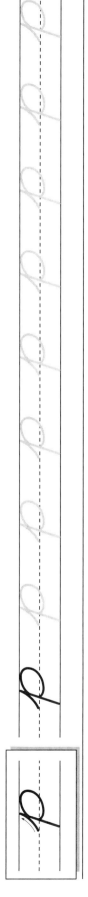

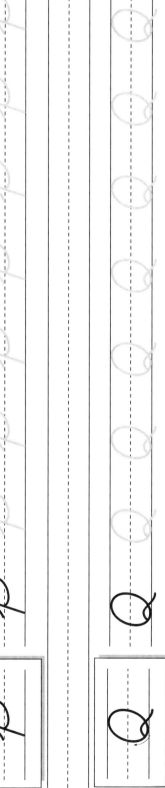

Quebec   Quin   Quito

Philadelphia, Pennsylvania

Name _____

V U

Trace and write the letters. Then write the sentences.

Aunt Violet lives in Vermont.

Uncle Ute lives in Utah.

Name _____ Date _____

w x

Trace and write the letters. Then write the words.

$\mathcal{W}$ $\mathcal{W}$

$\mathcal{X}$ $\mathcal{X}$

William Washington Wales

X-ray Xavier Xenia X-axis

Name _____

Date _____

Y Z

Trace and write the letters. Then write the words.

Yolanda Yukon Yorktown

Zena Zen Zachary Zimbabwe

Name _____

Date _____

Review

Copy the sentences. Circle your best uppercase letter.

The Lincoln Park Zoo is in

Chicago, Illinois.

The White House is

on Pennsylvania Avenue.

Is there space for a /o/ between words?

Name _____ Date _____

Taking Tests

In a writing test, you are sometimes given a prompt. Here is an example.

Prompt: The letters A and O are alike, but also different. Write a paragraph about how the letters A and O are alike and different.

Complete the paragraph that responds to the writing prompt.

The beginning stroke in both letters curves _____. The letter O, like A, is closed at the _____ line. A, unlike O, is not a round _____. O does not connect to other letters like A does from the _____ line.

Name _____

Date _____

Taking Tests

Use your best cursive handwriting to write a paragraph that responds to the writing prompt.

Prompt: The letters P and R are alike, but also different. Write a paragraph about how the letters P and R are alike and different.

_ _

_____

_____

_ _

_____

_____

_ _

_____

_____

_ _

_____

_____

_ _

_____

_____

Name _____

Date _____

Alignment and Margins

All letters should sit on the baseline and stay within the margins.

Four score and seven years

ago our fathers brought

forth on this continent a

new nation.

Copy as much of the sentence as you can within the margins.

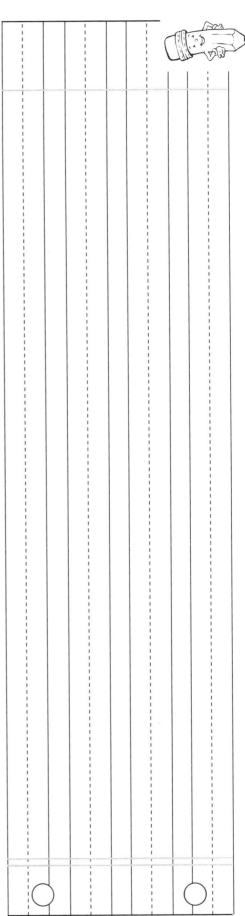

Make sure your writing stays within the margins of the paper.

Name _____

Numerals

Trace and write the numerals. Write the words.

1

2

3

4

5

one

two

three

four

five

6

7

8

9

10

six

seven

eight

nine

ten

Name _____ Date _____

Numerals and Math Symbols

Trace and write the math symbols.

$\$$

1

x

$\div$

$+$

$=$

Complete the problems.

$= 23 + 42 =$

$12 \times 3 =$

$\div 34 + 15 =$

$78 - 25 =$

$+ \overline{56 \text{ dollars}} =$

$\$ - \$ =$

$x \div \$ =$

$x + \$ =$

$\$ = \$ - \$ =$

$x \div \$ =$

Name _____

Punctuation

Repeat the patterns in lines 1 and 2.
Then write the sentences with correct punctuation.

??????????

?????????

Did you finish the puzzles

What a great idea that is

Yes, run as fast as you can

A Short Story
Copy the story and punctuate it correctly.

Farmer Fred worked all

alone One day a peddler came

by Look at this he said Wow

what an invention What could

the farmer do

Name _____ Date _____

A News Article

Copy the article on lined paper. Add correct punctuation,
including quotation marks.

Read All About It

Baytown, may 6 Scientists

have found a fossil of a

dinosaur heart They now

think that some dinosaurs

were mammals This is

amazing news said one

observer

Name _____ Date _____

Theme Paper

The last four lines on this page are without the dotted control lines.

Paper lined this way is called theme paper.

This is the paper you will use next year.

Copy the sentences.

Many states have state

trees and flowers.

Texas has the pecan tree and

the bluebonnet flower.

Name _____ Date _____

Transition to Two Lines

Write the sentences. In the last two rows, write the sentences without the guidelines.

A robin has many feathers.

An ostrich weighs 300 lbs.

Parrots know about 20 words.

Ducks lay eggs.

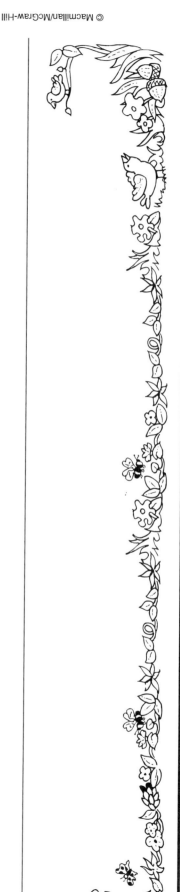

Practice with Small Letters

This is your first complete lesson without a dotted control line.

Write your letters and words the same way you have been writing them all year.

e u s n a i w m n o

see rain ox run mane

Sam was a curious raccoon.

He came across a fox.

Practice with Tall Letters

Practice writing tall letters and words with tall letters.

All tall letters should reach the top line.

t   d   l   k   h   b   f

fall   tall   doll   ball   kick

Tiff makes the best pet.

Jill likes to pet him.

Name _____ Date _____

A Report

Copy the report on lined paper.
Try to keep your letter height and spacing even without the middle line.

The Platypus

Is the platypus a mammal or a

bird? The platypus lays eggs. So do

birds. The platypus has a bill and

webbed feet. But it also has claws.

What do you think it is?

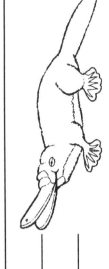

Name _____

Date _____

A Letter

Copy this friendly letter on lined paper.
Make sure the heading, closing, and signature line up.

264 Henry Street
San Francisco, CA 94109
May 3, 2003

Dear Joanna,

I can't wait to see you! We will
meet you at the airport on
Tuesday. Would you like to go to
the Exploritorium on Thursday?
We can take a picnic lunch.

Your friend,
Maria

Name _____   Date _____

Poster

Make a poster to help save Earth.
Write the information.

Plant a tree.
Save Earth!

Join the Plant-a-Tree Club

Contact: (Write your name,
address, and phone number.)

A Form

Pretend you are applying for a library card. Fill in the form.

Name:
Date of Birth:
Address:
Telephone Number:
Your Parents' Names:
Books You Like to Read:
Signature: _____ Date: _____

Name _____

Date _____

Name

Date